WEEKLY READER BOOKS presents

What Is a Rainbow?

A **Just Ask**™ Book

Hi, my name is Christopher!

by Chris Arvetis
and Carole Palmer

illustrated by

James Buckley

FIELD PUBLICATIONS
MIDDLETOWN, CT.

Well, let me show you.

As the sun's rays
shine through the prism,
the light is bent.
As the light bends,
it splits into many colors.

In the sunlight
there are many colors.

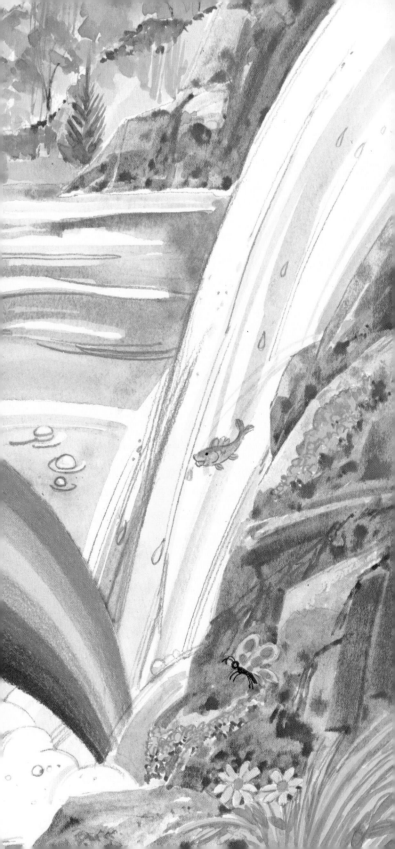

Let's go up into the sky
and look at the rainbow.

The sunlight shines
through the drops.
The raindrops are
like tiny prisms.
They bend the sunlight
and split it into many colors.

As we look into the sky, we see – –

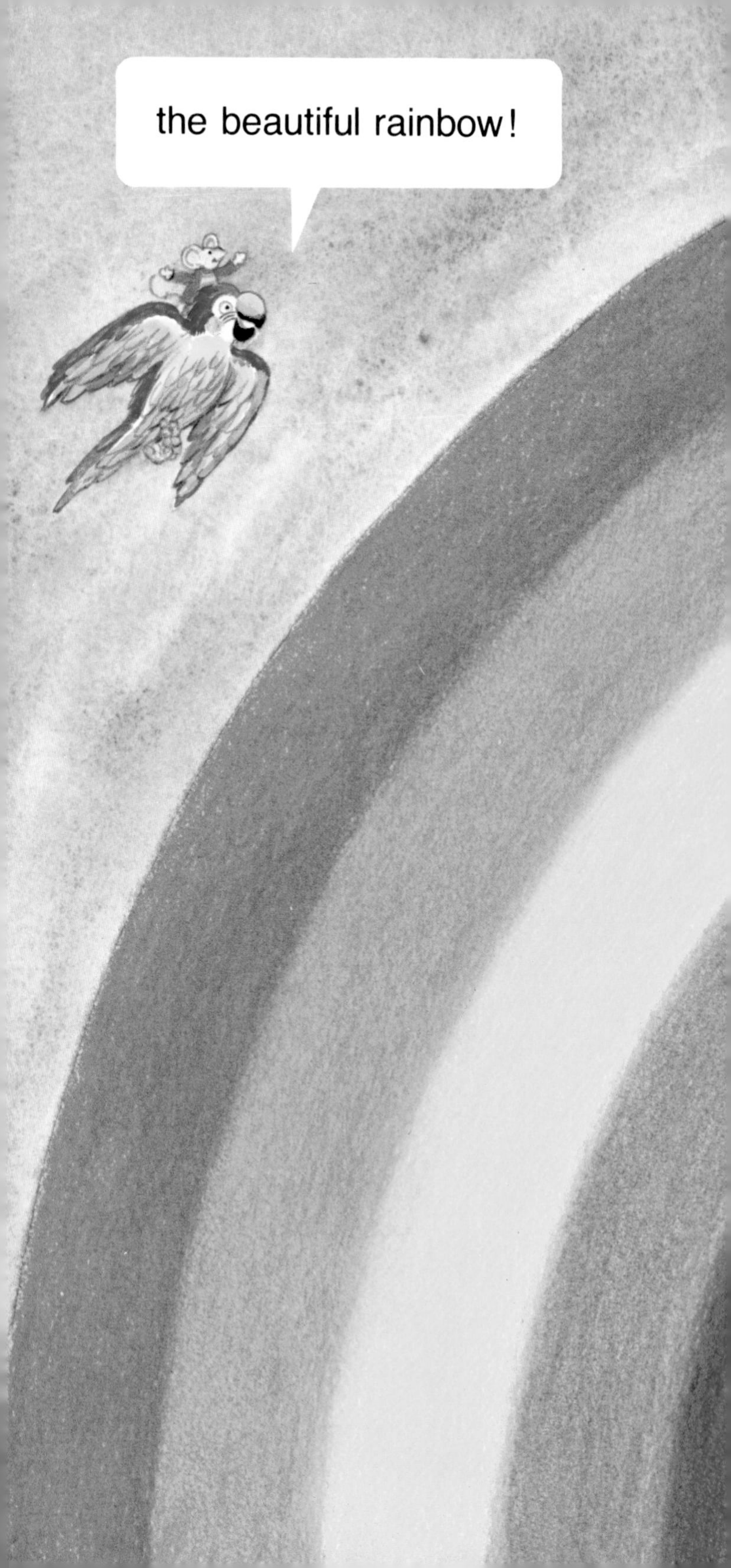
the beautiful rainbow!